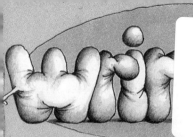

Published in the UK by
POWERFRESH Limited
Unit 3 Everdon Park
Heartlands Industrial Estate
Daventry
NN11 8YJ

Telephone 01327 871 777
Facsimile 01327 879 222
E Mail info@powerfresh.co.uk

Copyright :   Under License from Paperlink Ltd,
               356 Kennington Road, London SE11 4LD
               © Paperlink Ltd 2005

               Cover and interior layout by Powerfresh

ISBN 1904967108

Printed in Malta by Gutenberg Press limited
Powerfresh April 2005

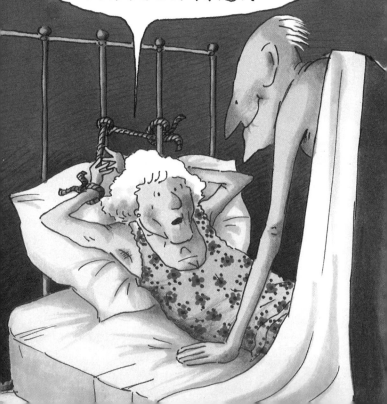

YOGA CLASS
TONI
IS YOUR OLD MAN COMING TO PICK YOU UP?
I HOPE SO, COS I CAN'T MOVE A MUSCLE
SILVEY JEX

HELLO...I'M YOUR BLIND DATE
ARE YOU? THEN HOWEVER DID YOU FIND ME?
URANT

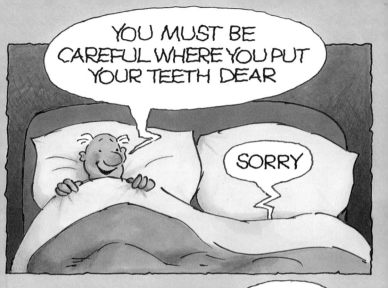

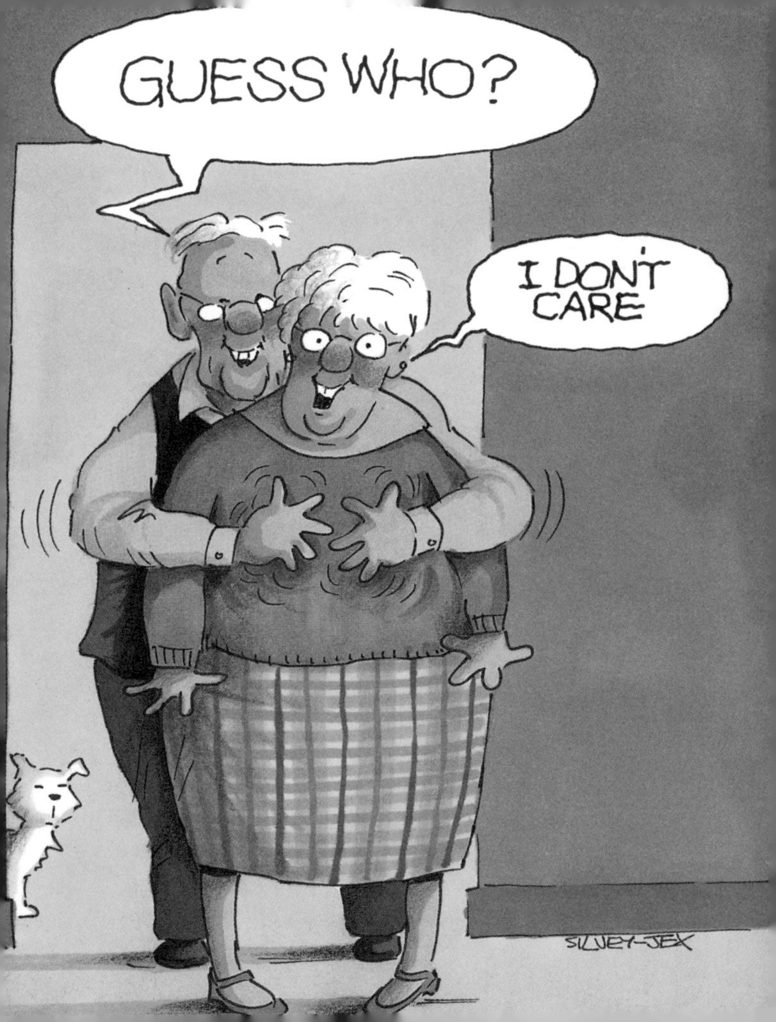
GUESS WHO?
I DON'T CARE
SILVEY-JEX

DID I HEAR CLICKETY-CLICK?
BINGO
YES. IT WAS MY RHEUMATISM
SILVEY-JEX

I'VE DEFINITELY LOST MY SEX DRIVE
WELL I HAVEN'T MOVED IT
SILVEY-JEX